THE SEXIEST GIRL EVER

CARMEN GARRETT

Table of Contents

Dedication

This book is dedicated to all the gay and lesbian (men and women) who really understand this particular lifestyle, and must know this lifestyle how one may become gay or lesbian, maybe this book, will enlighten someone with the knowledge of how your thoughts, feelings, and fears, of the lifestyle, will give you some type of peace and love towards them, because they are people too!! And the issues of what they deal with on a daily basis.

This book is to the memory of my dear cousin: Mr. Tommie Tucker Garrett

I miss you so, very, very, much!!!

Introduction

In today's society, people are in an uproar about being gay or lesbian. They even passed a law allowing gay and lesbian couples to get married, and have the same rights as any married man and woman today.

So society is saying what in the world is going on today, I don't know, but I do know for sure, you can't be born gay or lesbian, it's all learned behavior, I'm Carmen Garrett and this is my story.

Chapter One

The Birth Of Carmen Garrett

It all started, when a young couple in high school met for the first time, Jose Lopez and Maria Garret, he was eighteen years old, and she was sixteen years old.

He was a basketball star, a senior in his last of school with a scholarship on his way to college, and she was a track star, a junior in her third year of school, awaiting her scholarship to college.

One night after a basketball game, that Jose played in and Maria attended, they talked in the gym, Jose asked Maria to come and go with him to the local malt shop (canteen) a place where all the kids go and hang out, to dance, play, listen to music, and just talk to each other after school and sporting events, even on weekends.

They sat together and just talked for hours, Maria noticed that it had got a l1tile late and she needed to get home before she got in trouble with her parents being out late on a school night and all.

Jose said, I'll walk you home Maria, she said you would, thank you!!

He then smiled at her and she smiled back at him, they noticed that they liked each other, and was attracted to one another.

Then Jose asked Maria, do your parents allow you to date or go steady with boys yet!!

Maria replied, well yes!! Why do you ask, Jose!!

Do you want to date, and go steady with me!!

Jose replied, well yes!! I would, because you are fine!!

Maria thought about it, and then said okay!! Let's go steady!! But, don't you fool around on me with another girl, or I'm going to kill you.

Jose replied, okay, it's a deal, but let's seal it with a kiss, Maria says okay, but remember what I said, okay!!

Jose says okay, okay already, let's kiss!!

Maria says, kiss me then to seal our deal!!!

As there relationship grows stronger, with a day, they go skating, to the movies, house parties, after school dances, church, and back to the malt shop hangout.

They were falling in love and to really seal the deal I Jose tells Maria, I have something for you, and breaks out this big ring, and promises I Maria his love to her forever with what is called a promise ring.

Maria gets so excited about the ring I that she gives Jose a big wet juicy kiss right across the mouth I we call this a french kiss.

Then I she tells him that she has a surprize for him.

She takes him home I leads him into her bedroom I knowing that her parents are not home I and tells him to lay down across the bed as she lays down next to him and began to have sex.

It felt so good to them I that they did it over I and over I and over again.

Now I that Jose and Maria are a genuine couple I and a item I Maria has what she thinks is great news for Jose.

She tells Jose that's she pregnant with his baby!! And Jose says what!!!

Maria says to Jose what is right, and what are we going to do about it!!! Being in high school and all!!!

Jose thinks for a minute, takes back the promise ring, that he gave to Maria, then tells Maria that he'll be right back, goes to the local bank, where he's kept his savings, takes the money out of the account, goes to the place where he bought the promise ring, and then exchanges it for an diamond engagement ring to ask Maria to marry him.

When he came back to the place where Maria was she asked him where have you been!!! He proceeded to get on one knee, and said to her do you love you me, do you really love me, will you marry me!!!

Maria replied, I've had sex with you every week for the past six months, of course, I love you, and yes!!! I will marry you too.

So now there married Jose is in the united states air force military, he only stayed in college for two years, and didn't like it, plus thinking about a baby on the way puts weigh more pressure on your brain, than school.

Maria stayed and went to college at home and received her bachelors degree in education, and became a substitute teacher at one of the elementary schools.

One morning, while she was at home getting ready to cook breakfast, her water broke, and she had to be driven to the hospital.

She calls pepe her father, and explains the situation to him, he rushes right over, and speeds to the hospital.

When she arrives, tells pepe to locate and contact Jose and tell him what's happening.

Jose gets the news thru the american red cross, and gets permission from his superiors for leave, then heads to the airport, and flys home to the hospital.

As he arrives, he's immediately rushed to the emergency room to join Maria having a child, and giving child birth.

She's been in labor since twelve 0' clock noon, and now it's eleven 0' clock p. M. Fifty eight minutes later

Tomas Charles Lopez is born. Tomas, is lolbs, 9 ounces, 52 inches long an only child, no brothers or sisters.

Tomas spent most of his time with Maria, his mother, as Jose went back to the military to finish his tour of service with the air force, Maria and Tomas not only were mother and son, but they became best friends too, as he was just a baby, her pride and joy.

Maria did have an adult best friend from school, her name was nina, nina had two twin boys herself, and their names were le'roy and marvin, age three.

Nina and Maria took the boys everywhere, to the local mall, riding on the bus, and just walking down the street towards the local malt shop.

Tomas, le'roy, and marvin was always joined at the hip, traveling, when you see Tomas, le'roy and marvin wasn't far behind.

Tomas grew up playing games with Maria like dress up, wearing her wigs on his head, drying it in the hairdryer, he was fond of his mother's afro and long hair wigs, it made him look like a woman.

Putting on her fingernail polish, on his fingernails, and her lipstick on his lips he was fond of her ruby red lipstick.

Then it was time to put on Maria's clothes, first her silky satin skimpy see-thru short skirt, that only touched the top of her thighs, very sexy, and her very tight and skimpy booty shorts, Tomas tryied them both on but it didn't fit.

Tomas promised himself that he's going to do exercises to get his body in shape, and when he gets older he will be able to fit the dress and the shorts that he promises.

Maria thought Tomas looks cute in her wigs, lipstick, and clothes, even though the clothes didn't fit.

While, Jose was in nebraska, at the air base, Maria was afraid to sleep by herself at night, allowed Tomas to sleep with her, so she can sleep.

When Jose came home Maria put Tomas back into his own bed to sleep, now that Jose's home now, Maria can sleep, but Tomas being in his parents bed all of this time, couldn't sleep in his own bed by himself, because he was use to sleeping in his parents bed.

So Maria allowed him to sleep with she and Jose until he was sound asleep, Maria and Jose thinking Tomas was asleep, tried and did have sex together but, Tomas wasn't sleep all the way, could here them having sex together.

Tomas could here the moaning, and breathing, and erotic sounds, and the enjoyment of sex being performed by his mother Maria, he also able to see her perform oral sex on his father Jose, thinking all the time, these are the sounds and acts of women in love.

So Tomas thought this is what being a woman was like, the more he saw, and heard, and what it was to put on a sexy dress, sexy tight shorts, and high heel shoes, and flat heel tennis, wigs, and make up, what it is to be a woman, including what he was able to see his father do to his mother's body.

Tomas was a baby when he started sleeping in his parents bed, he's ten years old now, before he's back in his own bed, ten years in their bed, but, two of those ten actually knowing what was going on.

So Tomas went over leroy and marvin's house playing for long periods of time, having sleepovers, and campouts in the backyard.

You see Tomas body didn't look like a normal male body, le'roy and marvin had a normal male body at age 13, slender chest, slender thighs, slender legs, and a skinny booty, big lips, and a very big cocks.

Tomas body was already shapped like a grown woman's body at age 25, and he's 10 years old, would you like to say a coca-cola shaped body, where do we start, I know at the top:

Small head, big juicy lips, big chest with medium breast, now lets jump to the bottom, small tiny feet, skinny legs, slender athletic thighs, and a big phat apple shape juicy booty.

Leroy and marvin first noticed Tomas body real quick just as soon as he turned age 10, and really got turned on aroused and excited, about his lips, his booty, and his dick.

You see, leroy and marvin are gay, they love to have sex with boys, and especially men, they love to suck mens cocks, and have their booty fucked, and break in a young naïve boys, who don't know or haven't had sex with anyone (male or female), yet, and they wanted Tomas.

Their plan is invite Tomas over their house for a weekend sleepover, this weekend, and then each one of them will take turns fucking him, and sucking his cock, or they'll both will do it together, in hopes of turning him out and making him gay also, so they'll all be gay together, and be able to have sex with each other always, including Tomas.

So the next day, which was thursday morning, leroy and marvin asked their mother can they have a weekend sleepover starting tomorrow.

Nina said yes, but who's coming over, and the boys said Tomas, if you can asked his mother for his permission to come and stay over, and if he wants to come and stay this weekend.

Nina said, promise me that you'll do your homework, and absolutely, no horseplaying or clowning around in the house this weekend, okay, and the boys promised.

Then the boys said, hurry mom, and call Maria to get her permission for Tomas stay!!!

Leroy and marvin's plan was coming together with Tomas and what they plan on doing to Tomas, little did Tomas know what was in store for him this weekend.

Leroy then called Tomas on the telephone, hello Tomas, this is leroy, I want you to bring with you some little items of clothes when you come over, okay.

Tomas said, okay what!! Your mother's sexy short satin dress, her red tight silk booty shorts, her grey high heel shoes, her white body shirt with the letters she just made on them, her afro wig, her ruby red lipstick, and two pairs of her thong panties, what is this all for Tomas asked!! Leroy said, oh! We're going to play a game of dress up, then afterwards a new kind of game, the clothes and the rest of the things are for saturday afternoon and saturday night.

Now, it's friday, and Tomas, leroy, and marvin are all excited about the weekend.

Marvin tells leroy that, he's so wet between his booty cheeks, and his mouth is so juicy thinking about tonight and this weekend.

Leroy tells marvin to stop it, and remember, Tomas doesn't know about us yet!! But he will tonight and this weekend.

So here we are schools out leroy and marvin are finished with their homework, and it's time to have some fun.

Tomas arrives with his bag of clothes, especially the things leroy told him to bring.

Nina and Maria make a final check around the house before they leave for the weekend, remember what we said, and remember we'll be back sunday night, you boys have fun now.

It's five o'clock the boys began to watch a movie on t.V. And now it's eight o'clock and marvin ask Tomas a question: Tomas have you ever been kissed before, and Tomas says, why yes by my mother.

Then marvin said, I'm not talking about your parents, silly I mean from a girl your age, Tomas thought about it and then said no, not at all.

Marvin then said, we'll, do you want a kiss from me!!! Because I really want to kiss you badly, maybe as a experiment to see if we're attracted to each other, okay!! So Tomas said kiss me then!!

So marvin tells Tomas I'm going to show you how to kiss, but not just kiss, but french kiss me!!

So how does that feel, are you excited or aroused, if not lets try this,

Marvin then pulls down Tomas pants and underpants around his ankles, then tells Tomas to take them off.

Marvin then begins to hold Tomas cock and puts it in his mouth and begins to suck on it, and ask how does this feel!!

Tomas starts moaning, and moaning, and moaning and says it feels good, really good, marvin starts sucking even more Tomas starts yelling yes, yes, oh! Yes, then cums into marvin's mouth, Tomas calls marvin's name, marvin then says, my name ain't marvin anymore call me michelle!!!

Now, leroy who has been sitting on the couch, and watching Tomas and marvin this whole time, has his pants and underpants off rubbing his cock, getting excited and aroused.

Goes over to Tomas and tells him to bend over and spread your booty cheeks wide, takes the k-y jelly off of the dresser opens it sticks his hands inside of the jar, then rubs it all over his big cock, then tells Tomas this is a feeling that you've never felt before tonight.

He thens takes his large middle finger I forgot to tell you that leroy and marvin have large hands and fingers and jams it into Tomas booty hole, which makes Tomas yell out, ooooh!!!

Michelle starts back sucking Tomas cock again, while leroy is finger fucking Tomas with his big middle finger, as Tomas starts enjoying this and bouncing on leroy's hand.

Tomas bends over more, all the way over the edge of the couch, where you can see his entire big booty and booty lips looking like a phat juicy pussy.

Leroy then looks down at Tomas big phat juicy booty with Tomas booty lips just smacking at him; it was like they were blowing kisses at his cock. As leroy was pumping Tomas with his finger, he then takes his finger out of Tomas booty and slid in his cock.

Tomas has never felt this feeling before either in his life, Tomas stared yelling out very loudly, ooh!, Ooh!, Ooh!, Ahh!, Aah!, Yes!, Yes!, Yes! Leroy.

Leroy says, don't call me leroy, my name is le'ann and I'm about to fuck you with my personal, natural, big and thick dildo, which is attached to my body, girls call like me and michelle, call it a very big cock, and I'm about to fuck you good and hard with it deep inside your creamy colored juicy booty, and make you screem, and squirm, and squirt my cum out of it, when I cum really deep inside of you, so now what is Tomas to do!!

He's got michelle sucking his cock trying to make it cum one way, in front of him, and le'ann fucking him from behind another way, trying to cum, with moan after moan, after moan.

It's a feeling of arousal, excitement, enjoyment, and passion for Tomas, that's going on inside of him.

An sense of sexual awakening for him, thanks to le'ann and michelle, Tomas is starting to fill like them, at like them, and become what they are, with every stroke of le'ann's cock, and every suck of michelle's mouth on Tomas cock.

Their both trying to awaken the female side of Tomas, and allow him to become gay, to feel like a female, a woman, who will only love to have sex with boys and men.

So as le'ann strokes her cock inside Tomas, it's starting to have an effect on Tomas.

Tomas starts loving this feelings, as michelle sucks Tomas cock, Tomas starts to cum inside michelle's mouth and le'ann starts to cum, michelle swallows all the cum, as she's loving it. Afterwards le'ann and michelle ask Tomas, how does he feel now, Tomas says, that he wants to do it again, and again, and again, because he likes and loves this new game their playing, I to keep playing it, the whole weekend.

Le'ann and michelle says, Tomas we have more surprizes for you tomorrow, okay Tomas!! And Tomas says, sure!! Le'ann and michelle, but stop calling me Tomas, my name is Carmen now, Carmen Garrett!!!

And I'm the most beautiful, sexiest girl ever!! With the badiest body in the world, boys and men especially men, will want me to be their woman always, and the sex with them, will be ten times better than with you.

So now get over here, so I can make you cum all over me, because I've never had a cum bath before, and you two are going to give me one together, because you two made me, and your going to give it to me right now, I'm going to suck your cocks raw.

Because I'm Carmen Garrett!!! And I always get what I want!!

Chapter two

Carmen Garrett's Coming Out Party

It's saturday morning, and the girls wake up, take a shower and have some breakfast.

Afterwards, it's time to put on some clothes, le'ann and michelle decide on a white tee shirt, blue jeans, and white tennis shoes.

I'm sorry, le'ann and michelle, they have plain looking bodies, slender skinny legs, no chest, no booty, but they have very big lips, and no hair, giving you the impression of their biggest talent, they really do look like boys, for real.

And here comes Carmen, who is blessed with a whole head of hair, a goregeous figure, sexy legs

And a big juicy pair of lips, small waist, and a very big apple bottom juicy booty, she's very beautiful, for being a boy.

Wearing a black afro wig, ruby red lipstick, a red tight body suit with white letters saying, french kiss me, and I'll be yours, on the front, red thong panties, silky red booty shorts, and white flat slip-on tennis, very sexy.

Carmen asked le'ann and michelle, where are we going today, they said to the local shopping mall to shop for some good looking fine men.

Carmen said, my, my, my, look at all the fine men, here at the mall, are you all looking at us seeing how pretty we look, or just my shirt!!! Anyway here we are!!!

Then Carmen dropped her scarf on the floor, and bent over to pick it up, showing the men her perfectly shapped apple bottom booty, and winked at them, pointing to her shirt, and to the labeling that was on it, and yelled out "if you want, what I got I'm here, to give it away!! Le'ann and michelle said to Carmen stop it girl, before we get into trouble!!!

Later on that night, the girls dressed up to go out partying, le'ann and michelle both had on a black halter top, and a black mini skirt, with leggins and black leather boots.

Carmen wore her mother's white sexy short satin dress, this time it fit!!! It draped just right over her thighs, and a pair of white stilletto boots, with five inch heels, she was goregeous.

As they went club-hopping from club to club, le'ann and michelle started introducing Carmen to their gay and lesbian friends.

Carmen started being attracted to men and woman now, she french kissed both men and women, and enjoyed it so much the more as she invited them all to have sex with her, all at the same time.

As Carmen started coming out more and more with this different lifestyle, awakening to it.

Everyday she thinks she's female, all in her mind and with her body, even though she thinks, and acts, and talks and walks like a female.

She's really a male boy, thirteen years old, she was ten years old when she had her first sexual experience, as Tomas, but now she's Carmen, with the sexual experience and having this lifestyle for three years.

Having sex with too many people now, men and women, Carmen is sucking and licking cocks and eating pussies and loving every minute of it.

As Carmen reflects back to her childhood, now that she's thirteen and going strong, with her life, having sex with any and everybody imaginable.

She's an only child, who is very close to her mother, picking up all of Maria's habits: her walking, her talking, her jestures, the way she stands, waves her hand, the way she sits in chairs, they were like girlfriends, than mother and son, remember Carmen's a boy, Tomas is very intelligent for is age, and he can comprehend almost anything very quickly.

Tomas watches the way his mother and father acts together romantically or otherwise, the way his mother socializes with her other women friends, he picks up the way women are responded to when men are around them, instead of acting like a little boy should act.

Tomas chooses his alter ego Carmen, and chooses to act a teenage female girl.

Because that's how Maria his mother got lots of attention after having sex with Jose, Maria became the most popular girl in school and a bad reputation with that, and looking so angel like to boot, with all the other girls who had sex in high school.

So Carmen also wants to be and have that bad reputation in school too, being a bad girl one way, and angel like another way, getting rid of Tomas once, and for all in her mind, and having this goregeous body, to keep, that's hers and using it to her advantage.

When Tomas had sex with leroy and marvin for the very first time ever, leroy and marvin, knowing to like, date, and having sex with only men, and also being gay.

Puts Tomas in a very difficult position to be in, not ever knowing about sex, and not ever having sex before.

Tomas became excited, aroused, loved, and he enjoyed having this happen to him, experienced what it was like to be female, instead of male.

And his mind transferred over to the female part of him, rather than the male part of him, in the brain.

Well his thinking female thoughts, instead of male thoughts, and became what we now know as his alter ego, Carmen!!! With a female looking body to boot.

Carmen now enjoys being with, talking with, being surrounded around by, having sex with men, and loving everything that goes with it.

As Carmen's popularity grows, jealousy also grows, between her, le'ann, and michelle, after all Carmen is getting all the men!!!

But, do you blame Carmen, for what has happened to her!!!

It's not Carmen's fault, that all the men want her, she's beautiful!!!!

Le'ann and michelle did introduce Carmen to all of their friends and lovers, did they!!!

It's not Carmen's fault that all the men wanted Carmen, just for her shape and trying to fuck her all the time, due to her looks and she took advantage of them.

There were: james, jason, jimmy, jessie, and Johnny, michael, maury, and maurice, richard, rocky, randy, and rowland all trying to get a chance to fuck Carmen.

Maybe they wanted her all at the same time, and give her a cum bath, or to turn her into a nyphomantic, because she loved sex and men.

Since Carmen has been introduced to men, and they like that hot body and that juicy booty, young and tender.

It's been nothing but sex, sex, sex, and more sex, on the mind of Carmen lately!!!

Having sex at house parties in the basement, in swimming pools at pool parties, in the park, at strip clubs for men only, inside bathroom in night clubs, she's doing all of this at the young tender age of thirteen years

The movie they were watching was an x rated adult sex tape that leroy got from their uncle vernon.

Anyway, the movie involved a naked woman, and two naked men having sex together.

The two men put their cocks inside her, one man put their cock inside her ass, and the other man put his cock inside the woman's pussy.

And made her cum first, then they all came together, she then sucked both of their cocks together and made the men cum again together giving her a cum bath.

Carmen's the woman in the movie, le'ann and michelle are the men in the movie.

Le'ann and michelle are gay, and attracted to men longer than Carmen was, so (i.E.) Two men together having sex with a woman, (Tomas /Carmen) has a body of a female, so (he/she) thinks woman, so she (Carmen) thinks she a woman, so she is a woman.

And attending high school now, as a freshmen, one of the gay friends showed Tomas, how to hide his male cock and totally look like a real woman completely.

After knowing this Tomas becomes Carmen again, this time totally knocking Tomas mind out for good, becomes Carmen this time totally forever, and register for high school under the name of Carmen Garrett!!!!

Chapter three

Being Carmen Garrett

It's not easy being me, I have a beautiful, goregeous body, a beautiful head of hair, a small waist, a highly intelligent i. Q. Of 4.0 G. P. A.

But, all men want to do is to have sex with me, because of my good looks and goregeous body, where I am going to find time to be with them all!!

I'm only thirteen years old, an I'm receiving all of these telephone calls from men, my parents are going to start asking me questions about these men.

Who are they, where do they come from, how do they make their living, and what do they want from you!!

After all your only thirteen, and in high school, young lady, and not a 11tile tramp or a 11tile whore running around in the streets, Carmen says to her mother, okay mama!!

Carmen's thinking to herself, I may not be a 11tile tramp!! But a 11tile whore, that's up to debate!!!

I am having a lot of sex with men lately, but I have not reached the level of whore, yet!!!

Maybe, I ought to pursue a career in politics, with the lifestyle and reputation I desire, I'll have a lot of fun and go to a lot of parties at the nations cabinet bulding, I heard that the liberals, and conservatives, really know how to get freaky in Washington D. C.

Oh! Well, I've got four long years of high school just waiting for me, I think that I need to party between semesters.

And after school, also on the weekends, yeah!! But always after I do finish my homework, first, that's for sure i!!

So what kind of boys are in high school, their are freshman, sophmores, juniors, and seniors.

And who are going to teach me about the high school ways, the seniors, of course, I'll start with them, first!!

Okay, where should I start, with the football team, basketball team, volleyball team, or track team.

I really like football, I'll start with the football team, I wonder how many seniors on the team, I can score with first!!! Maybe all of them!!!

Carmen got chosen for the cheerleading squad on the football team at her school, and she's excited about doing something other than her studies,

She's finally going to get to show off her body and her skills in a non-academic way, and get the attention she's been dying for.

And the attention of the boys on the football team, she's been craving for also.

After practice, Carmen slips into the boys locker room, and hides in the shower, waiting on the boys to finish their practice and take a shower then she will be able to shower with them.

Carmen says, I'm about to have some fun very soon, and play my own football game with the team, I'll have my own monday night football party!!

As the boys enter the locker room and start taking their showers, they hear a "meow" sound, then a "purr" sound, Carmen then jumps out and say hi, guys!! How is it hanging!! The boys then said, "a little to the left side", and Carmen said, "i can see!! And big too ".

Carmen says, I'm hungry for some hotdogs and sausages, your kind of hotdogs and sausages with lots of sauce too!! She was talking to the football team.

Will you boys help me out, with my hunger problem please!!! My mouth is wet and juicy, for some of that meat to eat, if you know what I mean!!

Maybe I can perform a strip tease act for all of you!!! Yeah! Let's turn this locker room into a strip club, and I can be the main attraction.

She was the main attraction alright the only female so to speak (gay male) there, but the boys didn't know that she was really a he.

As she took off her cheerleader outfit her white blouse, her short skirt, and tennis.

Carmen left—her panties on, hiding her male member, so the boys couldn't see it or feel it,

When they started to grab her phat juicy booty.

As she jumped, and switched, and jiggled that booty around.

The boys started to get aroused and horney for some that juicy booty.

Carmen yells, are you boys aready for me to start the show!!! If so, lets go!!!

Now, how is Carmen going to get away with not exposing herself as a boy!! When the whole football team are down to just their undershorts!!!

Carmen takes her g-string panties, in the next isleway, she has to work fast or the boys will see her, and know that she's not a female (girl), but actually a male (boy) who is gay.

She puts her cock in the cover of the g-string (the part were your genitials lay), then folds it up around and ties it with the string part.

Then ties the string around her waist, having her cock and genitials right under her booty, actually raising her booty a little higher exposing her booty lips to the boys arousing them even more.

Then the boys got a mattress from the gym floor, and brought it inside the shower for Carmen to give the boys a nice little treat.

She waits, as all the boys came in, and surrounded her inside the shower.

She starts kissing them each on the mouth, then french kissed them, as they pat her on juicy booty.

She gets so excited after the boys gives her pats on the ass.

She then goes to the middle of the mattress, wiggles her big phat juicy booty, then starts humping her booty in front of them, spreads her legs wide bends over and says to the boys "come and get it"

The boys are really aroused and horney now, two of them come up to her, one gets behind her, and the other one gets right in front of her face.

One boy slides his cock inside her booty, and the other boy slides his cock deep inside her mouth.

Carmen starts fucking and sucking their cocks, as each of the boys starts stroking their cocks at the same time.

As the rest of the boys watched, they all lined up waiting to get their chance to get a piece of Carmen.

As Carmen is fucking and sucking the whole team, she moaning, and panting, squirming, and screaming in sexual enjoyment with the team (all eleven boys) as they to start cumming in her mouth, she says, mmm!!! Yummy!!!

It was ten games played for the season (five home) and (five away), each time Carmen ran out on the field to cheer, the team gave her a standing ovation, the other cheerleaders didn't understand why, just Carmen, but went along with it anyway.

After the football season, Carmen became the most popular girl in the school, again!!! This time college!!! But this is Carmen Garrett!!!

Chapter four

Carmen Garrett's College Days

Hello everybody, it's me Carmen, my big day has finally arrived I'm graduating from high school!! And I'm so happy!!!

That I've decided to go off to college, with an scholarship in cheerleading, can you believe it!!!

I guess that all my hard work in high school as a cheerleader on the football team really paid off!!

I have an undecided major, due to the fact that I don't know what I want to study yet!!

I'm thinking about all those freshmen, sophmores, juniors, and seniors in college!!! My!! My!! My!!

Me, Carmen, in college, as a cheerleader, cheering on a major college football team, wow! I just don't know what to say!!!

I guess I'll have to stay in one of the college dormatory rooms that all the girls stay in, not!!

I'm staying off-campus due to the fact that I need my space!!

And what about all the parties I need to give on weekends!!

And after semester is over!!! I need an apartment, I need to stay off-campus, yeah!!

I'll love having my own apartment, it gives me so much freedom, to do what ever I want to do, and need to do like parties!!

I know I'll have lots of visitors over, mainly boys!!! Some girls too!!!

I'll need help with knowing my way around campus, and of course, the college rules too!!!

I'll need some time to unwhine after a long week of classes and parties will be a must!!! Especially after the end of a semester!!

I've decided on what I will study, it will be in economics!!! After all, I love money, I need money, and I want to have lots of money, and make lots of money!!!

So go Carmen, and learn all that you can about economics, and you'll probably end up on wall street as a stockbroker!!!

We begin our football season at the university of missouri, nickname: tigers, (the college that recruited Carmen as cheerleader), in addition to the powerful, exciting, big twelve conference, football team winning it's no: 21, national ranking starting september 2011.

We draw our attention to our cheerleading squad, and their fabulous freshmen cheerleader sensation ms. Carmen Garrett.

Can Carmen duplicate her amazing feet in college, as she did in high school, as a cheerleader, and become as popular in college as she was in high school, we shall see!!!

Hi, guys!!! I thank you for allowing me to be a part of your team, as a cheerleader, I hope I can live up to the reputation that has followed me from high school to college here at mizzou, I hope to elevate my performance level even better here than I did at madison high!! So wish me luck, that I may score more times here at mizzou!!!

Oh! Hum! So here I am in columbia, missouri what a town, I still see the cows mooing in the fields, I'm sooo bored here!!!

So whenever I get board, I go barhopping!!

And try to stir up some action, let me see what's happening around the town tonight!! What parties are going on!!

As I go around the town, I can see, hey!! A strip club!! I know their's a party going on in here!!!

Hi bartender, give me a seven and seven with ice, and a seagrams wine cooler please!!

Let's see a identification card, how old are you anyway!!

Carmen says, how old do I look to you!!

The bartender says, I don't know seventeen!! Look at me, how old do you think I am, young lady!!

Carmen says, you look seventy years old to me!! But I'm twenty one years old, buddy!!!

The bartender says, we shall see!!! Yep!! Your i.D. Reads twenty one, okay!!

And old enough to drink, and drink often so stop messing with me, and my time, and serve me my drinks!!

As Carmen looks down at the end of the bar, she spots the teams quarterback, he's about six feet three inches tall, with a wide chest, a small waist, huge arms, big bicepts, thick thighs, big long legs, wide feet, and a tight butt too!! Really buffed!!!

Carmen asked, what are you doing here!! In the strip club!! Looking at the talent!! Or for some action!! Because action is my middle name!!! What's your name!!

He replied, Johnny jones, from hazelwood east high school, in saint louis, missouri (all conference quarterback).

Carmen told Johnny, like I said, if your looking for a good time!! Call me!! And I'll give you the time of your life!! So let me buy you a drink!!! Johnny replied, no let me buy you one!!!

As they both watch the striper's dance around them, Johnny asked Carmen, say do you want to get out of here, and get something to eat!!!

Carmen says, a free dinner, sure!!!

I'll take you to the best resturant in town, girl!! Carmen says, okay ii but afterwards, allow me to take you somewhere very special too ii my own special place!!!

Johnny agrees to the ultimatum, but still curious of Carmen's motives, to get him to be alone with her.

He's heard about Carmen's bad reputation with boys, but has never been completely alone with her.

At the resturant, Johnny and Carmen both order steak (well done), baked potatoes, green beans, with a salad, and ranch dressing, to top it off a bottle of red wine.

Who would have thought that a senior quarterback, and a freshman cheerleader would be on a mini date together after just meeting in a strip club I but that's Carmen Garrett for you!!!

After dinner I Carmen takes Johnny up to her apartment for a night cap I and says thanks for buying me dinner Johnny!!

Oh I it was least that I can do I considering you being a lady and all I Carmen!!

Why Johnny I thank you for calling me a lady I but I won't think I'm one after tonight!! Not after what I have in store for you I dear!! Says Carmen.

Here Johnny I have some more wine I honey!!

Oh! Johnny I my very special quarterback, it's time for my special surprise that I promised you I it won't take but just a minute for me to change I honey!!

Please!! Get comfortable on the couch I says Carmen.

Aren't you hot Johnny I with your sports jacket on why don't you take it off for me, please!! And your shirt I and your pants I and your socks and shoes too!!

Now I Johnny's only wearing his tee shirt and undershorts!!

Carmen says I here I come!!!

Carmen comes out of her bedroom wearing a pink see thru babydoll nitee, with her big brown eyes, lucious ruby red lips, small tiny waist, slender legs, small tiny feet, athletic size thighs, and her big phat juicy booty.

Which makes Johnny's cock get sooo aroused and hard, even thru his undrshorts!!!

Carmen sees his anormus cock growing thru his undershorts and says, wow!!!

And Johnny takes a long, long, look at her juicy booty, and also goes, wow!!!

Johnny, then pulls off his tee shirt, and undershorts exposing his giant cock, gets back on the couch, lies back as Carmen spreads his legs climbs on top of him, opens her mouth, and begins to suck on his big cock.

As she sucks, she takes his cock inside her mouth, she begins to go deeper and deeper, and faster and faster she goes.

Johnny starts feeling the sexual sensations of Carmen's oral examination of his cock deep inside her mouth.

He begans moaning, more and more, as he cums inside her mouth, she begins swallowing it!!!

Afterwards, Carmen says to Johnny, mmm!!! Yummy!!!

Johnny then tells Carmen to turn over on her knees, and spread her legs wide, as he slides his cock inside her booty lips i!!

It's a sensation that Carmen has never felt before sexually, as Johnny continues to stroke her over, and over, and over again.

She screams in total sexual satisfiaction, enjoying every stroke he gives her.

As he cums, Carmen goes oooh!! Yes!! As he releases inside.

Carmen tells Johnny, thank you for being my special quarterback, and I'm your special cheerleader for life.

The next day was football practice, and at practice just before the big game tomorrow, as the cheerleading squad practiced one particular cheer.

As the cheerleaders lifted Carmen above onto their shoulders, Carmen fell and broke her left leg, and was rushed to the hospital.

As she entered the emergency room for treatment the doctor asked Carmen if she could get upon the examining table and what had happened.

As Carmen hopped on the table, the doctor noticed a bulge inside of her uniform skirt.

Then told everyone in the examination room to leave except another female nurse.

She, the doctor and the nurse told Carmen to please take off your uniform.

Carmen replied, sorry doctor, "i can't do that".

The doctor asked Carmen again "miss I need you to take off your uniform please!!

Carmen said, again, "doctor I can't do it, because you'll discover my secret".

The doctor asked, "and what is this secret, that you don't want me to know".

Carmen told the doctor "I am a boy, I may look like a girl but I'm a gay boy".

I need your help doctor, in addition, to my broken leg being operated on, can you operate on my male member also, and make me a girl totally!! Please, will you do it for me!!!

I'm begging you, doctor, to please!! Please!! Make me female, a total female with a real pussy!!!

As the doctor sees Carmen crying, with tears running down her face, she agrees to operate on this special part of her!!

Awarding Carmen with the body, shes always wanted, a female body, now!!

Carmen will not just look female, and have boy's genitals that she was born with.

But, become female with all the parts of a female body, mind, completely!!!

This will take about a week to do, to prepare Carmen, in her mind, as well as her body for the operation itself.

No one will ever know that Carmen, was actually Tomas, a boy, except two (leroy and marvin).

Not even Tomas own mother (Maria) and father (Jose') will ever know that he's Carmen, that he's a she now, after this operation!!!

After this procedure Carmen, will be all woman, including breast, mind and body to match.

She'll be able to have sex, and fuck like any other female girl who likes to ride cock and suck them too!!

The doctor says I pray that she's happy in her decision, and live with this decision, because there's no turning back, once it's done, it's done.

It's a week now, and Carmen's still in the hospital the operations over with, and she's talking to the doctor about her very new exciting body, and the side effects of it!!

She sooo sexy now!! She has long black hair, big brown eyes, two double-d breast, big athletic thighs, slender legs, small feet, small waist, and a big phat juicy booty!!

This is how Carmen is looking, she as been given the nickname of "the sexiest girl ever".

Johnny visited Carmen in her hospital room, tuesday.

Hey sweetheart, how are you feeling!!!

Carmen says to Johnny, I'm very sore!! But, I'm

Glad to see you today baby, I enjoyed saturday night being with you!!

Johnny says, I'm glad to be of service to you!!!

Carmen says, are you still my special quarterback! Johnny says, yes I am!!

Johnny says, are you my special cheerleader!!

Carmen says, you know that I am!! Johnny, do you love me!! Do you really love me!!

Johnny says, yes I do!! I really do!!

Carmen says, so let's go steady!!

Johnny says, okay!! We're going steady!! We're boyfriend and girlfriend now!!

Carmen says, Johnny's my big man, yeah!!

Johnny says, Carmen, you know instead of going steady!! Let's go all the way, and let's get married sweetheart!! Will you marry me!!

Carmen says, oh! My god!! Yes, Johnny!! I will marry you!!

The next day, which is wednesday, Carmen is being discharched from the hospital.

Excuse me everyone, that helped me in my healing process, while I was here in the hospital "thank you".

Johnny and I are engaged to be married!!

He proposed to me, here in the hospital, yesterday and I'm just letting all of you know our plans, before I leave.

We haven't set a wedding date yet, we'll work on it after Johnny moves in with me into our apartment.

We'll put an announcement in the local and national newspaper!!

We have some more great news, Johnny's just won "the heisman trophy award", as quarterback, for all he's done in the big twelve conference at the university of missouri.

Reporters from all around the nation interview him and ask the same question!!

Johnny "whats in store for you next!!

He replies, in addition, to getting married to my college sweetheart Carmen Garrett, I've decided to enter the national football league draft, on monday, in new york!!!

During the n. F. L. Draft, Johnny gets a telephone call, he talks to the party on the other line, smiles, then hangs up the telephone.

And then, Johnny hears a very important announcement, the miami dolphins are on the clock, the dolphins hands the N.F.L. Commissioner a card, and it reads.

On behalf of the miami dolphins, the dolphins select, Johnny jones, quarterback, from the university of missouri, as their number one draft choice!! Congratualations Johnny!!!

So Carmen and Johnny are off to live in miami, florida as a member of the miami dolphins.

Johnny, as the newest member of the miami dolphins, as quarterback, he will have a lot of responsibility.

And Carmen Garrett, now engaged, soon to become a new N.F.L. Players wife, way to go Carmen, "you've done it again".

Chapter five

Carmen Garrett's Life

As a N.F.L. player's wife

News flash, one of the greatest operations in history occurred in columbia, missouri at barnes jewish hospital on september 1, 2011, by dr. Sharon watts, md., Internal medicine.

Reporters are waiting outside the hospital to get an interview with dr. Watts.

Doctor, doctor, how did you know that this operation will be as successful as it is!!!

Dr. Watts explains, well, I studied the procedure, and also had knowledge of it!!

I had a colleague of mine perform the same procedure in russia, and called her for some advice!!

This was the first successful operation performed in the united states, and it was performed by me.

Reporter asked, "doctor, where is your patient now!!

Dr. Watts replies, "please, no more questions on the subject!!

Meanwhile, at the new horizons missionary baptist church, in miami, florida.

The pastor says, do you Johnny jones, take Carmen Garrett, as your lawfully wedded wife, to have and to hold, for better and for worse" for richer and for poorer, until death do you apart!!

Johnny replies, I do!!

The pastor says, do you Carmen Garrett, take Johnny jones, as your lawfully wedded husband, to have and to hold, for better and for worse, for richer and for poorer, until death do you apart!!

Carmen replies, I do!!

The pastor says, by the grace of god, and jesus christ, and the holy ghost, and these witnesses, I now pronounce you husband and wife!! You may kiss your bride!!! Ladies and gentleman, I present to you Mr. And mrs. Johnny jones!!!

Congratulations to Carmen and Johnny, and your new life together, and the move to miami, florida!!

Reporters gather around at the church, and ask Johnny "what is it like being a quarterback in the N.F.L.!!

Johnny replies, fellas I just got married here, can this wait!! I haven't even thrown a pass yet, no have I had any practice time, or even gone to practice!! I guess it's great!!!

Carmen comes out the church, and says, Johnny come on it's time for us to cut the wedding cake!

Johnny says to the reporters, I'll tell you what, I'll let you come and film our reception okay!! But be nice!!!

The reporters say, hey Carmen, you sure look beauitful today, you look like a runway model!!

Carmen says, thanks guys, I don't mind you taking pictures of me and my husband, as long as it is in good taste!! Take all that you need and want, because I love it!!!

The reporters then ask Carmen, what are you going to do with your time, when Johnny plays at away games!!

Carmen replies, guess I'll contiue my college education here at the university of miami, get a job, and become an N.F.L. Cheerleader for the dolphins, if you don't know I use to be one!!!

Johnny asked Carmen "were you serious about becoming a dolphin cheerleader!

Carmen says, yes I am, I'm also going back to college to get my bachelor's degree, in journalism, this time and become a reporter!!

I figure, I have to do something, while your off playing football all over the country, especially away games!!

You know how bored I can get, I need some excitement, some activity, something to keep me busy!!

That's why I picked journalism, it's hard work, and it will keep me busy, plus being a dolphin cheerleader this will be very exciting for me!!

And we'll be on the same team supporting one another, and getting paid for doing it!!

Carmen says, so Johnny baby, "what do you think about my opportunity, do you want me to do this or not!!

Because the alternative will be, for me to just stay at home, and cook, clean, have babies, go shopping, and wait for you to bring home a paycheck every week, and you know that's not for me!!

Johnny replies, okay! Carmen, I'm sold on the idea, go for it!!

Who knows, this may be fun!!!

Carmen says, thank you baby!! I love you!!

Sweetheart, I just want something of my own, and do something for myself, and not just depend on you, to support us!!

Johnny says, come on I'm tired, let's go to bed!!

Carmen replies, tired!! We haven't had our marriage constimated yet!!

Meaning, we need to have sex!!

Alright then, we need to fuck!!

To really become a husband and wife!!

Baby!!!

So come on and give me that big phat hard cock!!

Johnny says, Carmen, don't you hurt me, sweetheart!!

Carmen says, oh Johnny! Now that your my husband, I must insist that you put your cock inside my mouth so I'll suck it, dry!! And swallow all your cum!! Dear!!!

Johnny reponds, just as long as I'll be allowed to slide my big phat hard cock inside your phat juicy wet pussy, and make you cum!! Dear!!!

Carmen reponds, okay! Now it's time to go to bed!! Baby!!!

Johnny says, yes!! Let's go to bed, dear!!

News flash, today Carmen Garrett jones, becomes a member of the miami dolphins cheerleaders!!

Can this college superstar sensation be a sensation in miami, we shall see!!!

Reporters reply, hey Carmen!! Did you actually try out for the cheerleader squad or did you get it due to Johnny being quarterback!!

Carmen says, fellas I beg your pardon, I tried out on my own, for this position all the way, without no special treatment or iNFLuence!!

And plan to be one of the greatest, maybe the greatest miami dolphin cheerleader ever!!

The reporters reply, won't that make the other cheerleaders, and the players wife's jealous.

Carmen responds, you know, I don't care, if their jealous or not.

I'm doing this for my family, myself, and my career.

I want to become "the sexiest girl ever" okay!!

And I can't do it staying at home, baking cookies, cooking, and cleaning, and having babies!!

Ladies and gentleman, here's your miami dolphins football team!!

Featuring their sensational number one draft pick, quarterback, Johnny jones!!

And here comes your miami dolphins cheerleaders!!

Featuring their super sexy cheerleader sensation, Carmen Garrett jones, as captain!!

Give me a c, give me a—a, give me a r,

Give me am, give me a e, give me an,

Give me as, give me a c, give me a-a,

Give me an, give me ad, give me a y,

What does it spell!!

Carmen's candy!!, Carmen's candy!!, Carmen's candy!!, (It's finger licking good)!!

It's halftime at joe robbie stadium in miami, florida and the dolphin cheerleaders just left the field, with there sexiest looking cheer yet, "Carmen's candy".

It really caused a stir at the football game today with their uniforms on so tight and their halter top blouse and bikini shorts with pompoms!!

These uniforms with their cheer is not for the family, it's more of a striper's showcase of cheerleaders!!

And it's on television in front of a national audience!!

The onwer says, who's responsible for this!! Carmen Garrett jones, sir, the captain of the cheerleaders!!

The owner says, "find her, and bring her, to my office"

Mrs. Jones, please sit down, Carmen I know that your new to the team, but, their are rules to this game, that you must know.

Carmen says, Mr. Robbie, did I do anything wrong at the football game!!

Mr. Robbie says, Carmen, football is a family game, you cannot go around in those kind of kind of outfits, and cheer those kind of cheers!!

It effects the mothers and children that come and see the football game in person!!

The halftime show has to be family oriented, not whorish, football is not just a man's game anymore, but it's designed for woman, little boys and girls too of this great nation that we have.

Try to be a little more objective the next time in your cheerleading I please!!

Thank you, Carmen!!

Carmen says I'm sorry Mr. Robbie to have cause such an uproar at the halftime show!!

You see I'm use to a lot of men around me, and the kinds of shows I do, are for their benefit, to arouse them up so to speak!!

Let me show you the new cheerleader outfits anyway!! I'll think that you'll like them!!

Let me try one on for you I joe!! It's cute!!

Mr. Robbie says I no! No! No! You don/t have to try it on, Carmen!! I believe you!!

Carmen says, are you afraid of me showing you a little skin, or are you afraid of looking at my sexy body!!

Are you afraid of your wife coming in and finding me in your office, in this skimpy uniform showing off my belly button for you!!

Hey Mr. Family man, I know your the boss, but, bosses do fool around on their wives too!!

I know for a fact that that you've been seen running around with cheerleaders from the football team!!!

Mr. Robbie says, Carmen, where did you find out this information!!

Carmen said, I have my sources!!

Mr. Robbie said, my god!! You've only been in this town a little over two or three weeks, and you know my business!!

Carmen says, this is a part of my job also, being a reporter!!

What do you think of my additional job!!

Carmen says, this is my chosen profession, being a reporter, and a cheerleader, and going to college for journalism.

Mr. Robbie says, I'll have you thrown off the cheerleading squad, and out of my stadium, and fired!!

If it wasn't for the fact of your husband Johnny, and your advertising of Carmen's candy!!

That candy is a little money maker and the kids love it, and it's good for the community!!

Carmen, this is a good idea "Carmen's candy" when can you start production on it!!

Carmen says, we the cheerleaders, and the player's wives can start on it right away!!

But I'll need some financing from you, sir!!

You know advertising and production costs!!

Your iNFLuence with the girls and wives, will help me, I mean us, out tremendously with this project!!

Carmen says, okay ladies let's make some candy, were going to use as molds my body!!

From top to bottom, I want you to make a mold of my breast, my lips, my booty, and of course, my pussy!!

These candies are for the adult male population of miami and the united states!!

And every man from seattle to dallas, from dallas to new orleans, from new orleans to washington d.C., From washington d.C. To miami, all will know after these candies sell, that I am "the sexiest girl ever".

So let's stop for now, and let's go party!!!

The next day, which is saturday, Johnny says, hey, look what the cat dragged in!!

Where have you've been, Carmen my love!!

Carmen says, out partying with the girls!!

Johnny says, all night!! It's six o'clock in the morning!!

Carmen says, all we've been doing is drinking, and dancing, we forgot what time it was!!

Johnny smiles, yeah! Until you all saw the sun come up!!

Carmen says, oh! Johnny, don't be to angry with me, okay!!

I've got a real bad headache, and I need some sleep!!

Johnny says, well sleep fast dear, because we've got a afternoon football game today!! And all players, including cheerleaders need to be there at one o'clock sharp!!

Carmen says, a football game, today!!

Johnny says, it's saturday, you know!!

Carmen replies, but, I thought that football games are always played on sunday!!

Johnny says, they are played on sundays, but, this is pre-season dear! That means saturday football.

Carmen says, oh!! No!!

Johnny says, you go on and get some sleep, and I'll wake you up at noon!!

Welcome to the national footlball league, you just picked a bad night to party, you don't party before the game, you party after, remember that next time.

Carmen says, okay! Ladies lets get ready to shake some booty, and show some skin today, we're going to give the fans a real good show!!

The kind of show that men will want to have sex with their wives, and wives will have sex with their husbands, boyfriends, will want to have sex with their girlfriends!!

She's a very freaky girl, the one you don't take home mother, she'll never let your spirits down, once you get her off the streets.

She likes the boys in the band, she says I'm her all time favorite, she's alright, she's alright, that girls alright with me, hey! Hey! Hey! Hey!

Shes a super freak, super freak, shes super freaky, wow!!

That was your miami dolphins cheerleaders and their halftime show!! And what a show!!

The Miami Herald reports, are the miami dolphins selling football or sex!!

With the new halftime show between half's, the miami dolphins cherrleaders come out at halftime in these skimpy short uniforms not even covering up their bodies!!

Exposing our little boys and girls, and mothers to a erotic display of cheers, during a football game nationwide!!

"What are they thinking, who's running the stadium down at joe robbie".

Mr. Robbie replies, I rest assure you that I'll get to the bottom of this mess!! I guarantee it!!

Football!! Is an american sport, a family game, it's not just for the adults only! But, for kids too!!

I run a respectable stadium here, it's all about the football game!! Thank you!!

Mr. Robbie says, find Carmen Garrett jones, and get her little booty in my office, now!!

Here she is sir!!

Carmen, my sweet didn't we have a conversation concerning your cheers, in the halftime show!!

Carmen says, yes sir!! Didn't you like the new cheers, didn't it attract all of the men in the stadium!!

I know for a fact, that all the men in the stadium, including the football team, loved the halftime show!!

It's the number one halftime show in the united states!!

Look at the numbers around the N.F.L. We've got the number one rating of all the halftime time shows in america!! Isn't that great!!

Mr. Robbie replies, are you serious, about our numbers, well that's terrific!!

Carmen says, so what really is the reason, that you want to talk to me about, Mr. Robbie!!

Mr. Robbie says, oh!! Nothing!!

Carmen says, Mr. Robbie, I still think that your a very handsome man!!

Do you want to take me out to dinner sometime of course, it will be a business dinner!!

Mr. Robbie says, of course, a business dinner, let me think about it, and I'll get back with you, Carmen!! Have a good day!!

Just then, a movie director sees Carmen, excuse me miss, are you Carmen Garrett jones!!

Carmen says, yes I am!!

My name is simon west, I'm a movie director, and I have seen both of your halftime shows!!

I've seen you do those erotic cheers, would you be willing to take a screen test for me!!

Because I loved those cheers!!

Carmen reponds, really!! Why yes, I'll love to go with you, and take a screen test!!

Maybe, I'll become an actress, or even a movie star!! Wow!! Let's go!!

Carmen has done it, again!!!

Chapter six

Carmen Garrett "Movie Star"

The director says, now Carmen just come right in and sit down, this won't take long, have you've· seen or taken a screen test before!!

Carmen says, no! But I've seen one done, when I was a little girl on vacation visiting my grandmother in mexico.

The director says, don't be afraid of the camera just say these lines: oh! Bradley, since you've got stuck on bandaids, please don't have the bandaids get stuck on me!!

Carmen says, because I have a cut on a very indecent spot on my body, that's sensative to the touch, and it will tickle if you touch me there!!

The director says, that's very good Carmen, you've done well!! I'll call you soon!!

Carmen says, thank you, Mr. West!!

As Carmen gets home she walks in the door.

Carmen says, hi honey, I'm home.

Johnny says, where have you've been all evening!!

Carmen says, guess what!! I've been at a screen test for a part in a major movie!!

Johnny says, what!! A movie!!

Carmen says, yes, a movie, I'm going to become an actress!! Just as soon as the director calls me back!!

Johnny says, well, well, well, so my little Carmen is going to become an actress!! What is the world coming too!!

What are you going to do with your cheerleading and journalism careers!!

Carmen says, well I'm gonna have to quit!!

Johnny says, and what about your candy making project!!

Carmen says, that's gone too!! I have to put all

My effort into my acting career now!! I can see me now, Carmen Garrett jones, moviestar!! Money, money, money, money, and more money!!

Johnny says, I'm curious, what is the name of the movie that your suppose to be in, if you pass the screen test!!

Carmen says, it's called "the sexiest girls ever"

Johnny says, and who's all starring in this movie!

Carmen says, angelina jolle, charlize theron, gretchen mol, drew barrymore, megan fox, angelina martinez and me, Carmen Garrett jones!!

Carmen says, we should start rehearsal and receiving our parts as soon as I hear back from
The director, on october 7, 2011.

News flash, Carmen Garrett jones, that college sensation that stole the hearts of the big twelve conference, that became a superstar cheerleader of the miami dolphins!!

Is now gone hollywood, and become an actress in the upcoming movie "the sexiest girls ever"

Starring: angelina jolle, charlize theron, gretchen mol, drew barrymore, megan fox, angelina martinez.

Is erotic tale of women gone bad, and earning money the only way they know how, in the oldest profession known to women!!

Here in miami, florida we wish her all the luck, and great success in her new career!!

The diector says, okay! Carmen, lets take it from the top!! Lights, camera, and action!!

Carmen says, oh! Keith, don't you like me! I know you want me, baby! It's only one hundred dollars, for a few hours of fun!! Come on a give it to me!!

Keith says, okay! Baby, here you go, now lets go and have some fun!!

The director says, and cut!! Print!! That's beautiful you two are a natural, the best, that's a wrap, thank you!!

Hey sexy lady, you look like, you've been acting for awhile, you really are a natural!!

Carmen says, I just get into the part I'm playing and just role with it, that's all, nothing serious!

Angelina says, hey! Carmen, do you want a ride home with me!!

Carmen says, sure!! Lets go!!

Angelina says, so what made you get into acting and become an actress!!

Carmen says, well, I was coming out of joe robbie's office, one day, and bumped into simon west, the movie director, in the hallway, and he said he saw the halftime show at the football

Game, and liked it, and wondered if I would like to become an actress!! I'll have to do a screen test first!!

Angelina says, that's simon for you, it's fun becoming an actress isn't it!! And don't forget all the money!!

Do you want to come and see where I live, and get a drink or something, and we can continue to talk!!

Carmen says, sure!! I really do need a friend, I don't have any!! And also a drink too!!

Angelina says, I'll be your friend, and you can be mine, and maybe after we get to know one another well, girlfriends!!

So come on, and make yourself at home!

I'm going to change into something a little bit more relaxing, and I'll be right back!!

Do you swim at all!! I've got another bikini, that you can wear, we can go swimming together in the pool out back!!

Carmen says, you have a pool!! Cool!! And yes, I can swim!!

This will be fun, hey! Angelina, I love your mansion, it has so many rooms, I know your glad that you don't have to clean them.

Angelina says, I do have a maid!!

Here try this on, it should fit you!!

Carmen says, this is very pretty!!

Angelina says, Carmen you are a very sexy girl, from your luscious lips, your big juicy breast, your small tiny waist, your big phat booty, and your phat wet pussy!!

I really want to fuck you, really hard and eat that phat pussy and make you cum inside of my mouth, so I can taste your sweet juices!!

Please let me be allowed to make love to you my sweet!!

Carmen says, but were married women, and we have husbands to satify!!

I never was attracted to women before or even had sex with one!!

Angelina says, once you have been with a woman, you'll never won't to go back to a man again!!

No one knows a woman's body like another woman does sexually, or can make your pussy cum faster that a woman can, after licking it!! So let me fuck you real good!!!

Carmen says, okay!! Go for it!! But lets go swimming first!!

Angelina says, this is what a female actresses do for fun, in the acting industry!! So you beiter get use to it, Carmen!!

From ms. America to mrs. America, from the fashion magazine models to the runway models, from erotic actresses to major moviestars, all of them have sex with each other, and their all women!!

So Carmen you beiter get use to having sex with and liking women!!

So Carmen, kiss me, and let me french kiss you, in the mouth!!

Now, let me suck on your hard nipples, I'm sliding my tongue down your belly button towards your pussy!!

Now, spread your legs wide, so I can slide my head between them, so I can slide my toungue inside your wet pussy!!

I'm licking it up and down, sliding my tongue in and out of it!!

Making you quiver, shake, and moan, and cum inside my mouth!!

Mmm!! You do taste sooo good, your juicies inside my mouth!!

Carmen says, oooh!! Oooh!! I'm cumming!! Hard!! Angelina!!

Knock!! Knock!! Knock!!, Angelina!! Are you in you in there!!

Angelina says, who is it!!

Lucy says, it's me dear, Lucy!!

Angelina says, lucy! We're out back in the swimming pool!!

Lucy says, what in the world!! What are you two doing in there!!

Can I going in, please!!

Angelina says, this is Carmen, Carmen meet lucy!!

Carmen says, hi!

Lucy says, h!! Can I eat and lick your pussy too!!

Carmen says, sure!! I don't mind!!

Angelina says, you, are!! I also want Carmen too

Is that alright with you, lucy!!

Lucy says, okay! I guess!! Just as long as I can be Carmen's girlfriend, as well!!

Carmen says, sure!! I don't mind, if lucy becomes my girlfriend!!

Who would have thought it, I all I wanted was a friend, female wise, and now I have two girlfriends!! Wow!!

Angelina says, alright enough talking, lucy get over here and start eating Carmen's pussy!! And mine too!!

Lucy says, okay! Here I cum!!!

Carmen says, oooh! Oooh! Yes!! Yes!!, Eat my pussy!!, Eat it, eat it, I'm cumming, lucy!!!

Lucy says, mmm!! Mmm!! Sooo!! Good!! Your sweet pussy juice!! You've got a very sweet pussy, Carmen!!!

Angelina says, Carmen, before you go, we need to tell you something, you know this makes you a lesbian now!!

Lucy says, yes, you are a lesbian!! Carmen says, yes, I know that's why it's difficult for me to go home now!!

I'll need you both to really stick to your word about loving me!! I'll need your love!!

As Carmen gets home, she starts packing her clothes and gathering her things up for a final goodbye and moves into angelina's mansion for her new life as a lesbian, and the lesbian lifestyle

Johnny comes home and finds clothes and things of his wife, gone!!

As he looks around the house, he says, Carmen, Carmen, are you here!!

As she comes inside the house, she sees Johnny sitting on the couch drinking a beer!!

Carmen says, oh! So your home Johnny, I need to talk with you about something!!

Johnny says, where are all your clothes, and things, Carmen!!

Angelina says, we'll have to go to the premier which opens this friday and nationwide saturday!!

Let's make a toast to the priemier, and the opening, may it make us lots of money!!

Lucy says, here!! Here!!

Carmen says, here!! Here!!

Well girls I have to go now, there's sometimes I need to do!!

You two do love me, don't you!!

You are my girlfriends, right!!

     Carmen Garrett: The Sexiest Girl Ever

Lucy says, yes, that's for sure!!

Angelina says, yes, that's for sure, definitely!!

Carmen says, okay!! Then!!

Carmen says, their at a friends house!!

Johnny says, why!! What's going on!!

Carmen cryies, I'm not in love with you anymore, I want a divorce!!

Johnny says, why!!

Carmen cries, I've found someone else that loves me the way I need to be loved, more than you can!!

Johnny says, who is it that loves you more than me!!

Carmen cries, her name is angelina, she makes me feel more alive than any woman has ever done before, I am a lesbian now, and I love with women!!!

Johnny says, I guess that leaves me totally out!!

Carmen says, I didn't mean for us this to happen, it just did!!

Please, take care of yourself, Johnny!!

Johnny says, don't worry I will!!!

Take care of yourself too!!!

Carmen says, I will!!! I guess it's time for me to leave now.

She walks over to Johnny gives him a french kiss in the mouth, walks down the steps to angelina's suv, turns around looks at Johnny then gets inside, and then angelina starts the suv and takes off.

Angelina says, Carmen are you alright Carmen says yes!! Lets go home!!

Johnny became the NFL's all time leading passer with over five thousand yards, in a single season, the miami dolphins won their division, the conference title, and the super bowl.

The movie "the sexiest girls ever" became an overnight success of the weekend grossing over twenty million dollars in a single night!!

For the role in the movie, Carmen became the biggest acting actress in america, starring in several other movies, she's now the biggest "moviestar" in the world.

Carmen and angelina went on to get married, that next saturday, lucy, still visits them on the weekends!!

What a life for Carmen Garrett born, Tomas Lopez, a boy who became gay, was made female by an operation, who got married to an NFL quarterback, became lesbian, and married another female actress, and became an overnight "movie star" . . . . Our little miss Carmen Garrett.

www.ingramcontent.com/pod-product-compliance
Lightning Source LLC
Chambersburg PA
CBHW040741150726
48196CB00060B/1474